Found:
GOD'S WILL

John MacArthur, Jr.

VICTOR BOOKS®

A DIVISION OF SCRIPTURE PRESS PUBLICATIONS INC.
USA CANADA ENGLAND

Unless otherwise noted, Scripture quotations are from the *King James Version*. Other quotations are from the *New American Standard Bible* (NASB), © the Lockman Foundation 1960, 1962, 1963, 1968, 1971, 1972, 1973, 1975, 1977. Used by permission.

Former title: *God's Will Is Not Lost*

Library of Congress Catalog Card Number: 77-3816
ISBN: 0-88207-503-9

17 18 19 20 Printing/Year 94 93 92 91 90

VICTOR BOOKS
A division of SP Publications
        Wheaton, Ill. 60187

Contents

1

Is God a Cosmic Killjoy?

As I travel around, one of the questions I am asked most often is, "How can a Christian know the will of God for his life?" Most of us acknowledge that God has a plan for the life of every believer, but often there seems to be some trouble in finding just which way this plan goes at a particular juncture. There are plenty of books, pamphlets, and sermons hitting at the problem, and yet the answers sometimes seem to elude even the most persistent searcher. My prayer is that this little book will help fill in some of the gaps in a fresh and very practical way.

One may look for definite guidelines in this area but merely wind up with a variety of ideas.

Some apparently think that God's will is lost. At least they say they are searching for it! To them, God must appear to be a sort of divine Easter bunny who has stashed His will, like eggs, somewhere out of sight and sent us running through life trying to find it. And He is up there saying, "You're getting warmer!"

Others offer the suggestion that God's will is to be found via a traumatic experience. Running down the street, you fall on a banana peel and land on a map of India. Immediately you say to the Lord, "Thank You for that clear leading. I understand! India it is!" Or there is always the voice out of heaven or the vision in your dreams calling you to Chile.

Then there are those who are actually afraid of the will of God. I will never forget the athlete who came up to me at Hume Lake Camp and said, "I'm not sure I want to give my life to Jesus Christ because I am afraid of what He will make me do." He had the idea that God wants to take robust athletes, break both their legs, and make them play the flute. This implies that God is a kind of "cosmic killjoy," stomping on everyone's fun and raining on parades. People with this view actually fear the will of God as a severe way of life which will demand the sacrifice of their most treasured ability or possession.

Then there is the brass ring mentality. Remember the old merry-go-rounds with the brass rings? There are Christians who see God's will like that: It's nice if you get the brass ring, but if you don't, just settle for the iron one. In other words, don't really run to win—just be in the race.

I have read in some sources that the will of God is the "fortuitous conjunction of circumstances and impulses."

And so the theories go on.

In the middle of this muddle we still ask, "What is the will of God? Are there any concrete principles which may be simply stated and actually put into practice?" I believe there are! That is the point of this whole book. Can you know what job to seek, what school to attend, what girl or guy to love, what decision to make in any given situation?

Yes. You no longer have to worry. The struggle is almost over, the search almost done.

Let's begin with a simple assumption. Since God has a will for us, He must want us to know it. If so, then we could expect Him to communicate it to us in the most obvious way. How would that be? Through the Bible, His revelation. Therefore, I believe that what one needs to know about the will of God is clearly revealed in the pages of the Word of God. God's will is, in fact, very explicit in Scripture.

As we look at some biblical principles in the

following pages, be prepared for an unexpected and surprising conclusion that could change your life.

2

The Crucial First Step

The will of God is no longer a problem to me—and it need not be one to you either. Let's begin at the beginning and see what God has to reveal to us through His Word.

The Apostle Peter introduced to us the concept of the will of God. Throughout his second epistle, Peter warns us about false prophets, whom he calls "wells without water" and "dogs returning to their vomit." Peter says that it is characteristic of these "wells" (which would seem to be sources of life-giving water but are not) or these "dogs" (who go back and lick up the vomit of their own once-forsaken sins) to deny two things. First, an apostate or false teacher denies the deity of Jesus Christ, denies "the Lord that bought them" (2 Peter 2:1). The second thing that an apostate denies is the second coming of Christ (2 Peter 3:1-10). In mockery he says, "Where is the promise of His coming? All of you fanatics are running around saying that Jesus is coming. Where is He? I don't see Him." He reasons on this basis: "Since the fathers fell asleep, all things continue as they were from the beginning of the creation." He says, "Nothing will ever change, for it never has. I will never die. I never have. I couldn't possibly get cancer. I never had it before."

Peter said, "You forgot about the Flood. All things haven't continued as they were." And they are not going to continue as they were! God is going to intervene in a great fiery judgment (v. 10). "The Lord is not slack concerning His promise" (v. 9). In other words, just because we don't see God invading the world in judgment, it doesn't mean that He can't! It doesn't mean that He made a promise and won't keep it. His delay doesn't mean that He is either impotent or unfaithful, but that He is long-suffering, "not willing that any should perish but that all should come to repentance" (v. 9).

This is the first thing about God's will—He wants men to be saved. So much so that He stays His judgment. Paul said, "For this is good and acceptable in the sight of God our Saviour;

Without Christ, man is a stranger to God. He is a rebel against God, a foreigner in God's universe.

The Bible says that God's will is that men be saved, and that is where it all starts. Jesus made this clear in Mark 3:31-35. He was already teaching inside a building when His brothers and mother arrived. The multitude was sitting on the inside, and it was so crowded that His family could not get to Him. Someone said to Him, "Jesus, Your mother and Your brothers outside seek You."

He answered, "Who is My mother, or My brethren?" (v. 33)

I am sure the crowd's reaction was something like: "What kind of question is this? Everybody knows His mother and brothers!"

If Jesus' first reaction did not shock them, His next words did. "He looked round about them which sat about Him, and said, 'Behold My mother and My brethren!'" (v. 34)

Each person probably looked at the other and thought, "Who, me?"

Then he qualified it. "For whosoever shall do the will of God . . . is My brother, and My sister, and mother" (v. 35).

What was Jesus saying? He was teaching that in order to be related to Him, one has to do the will of God. Turn it around. To do the will of God one has to be related to Jesus.

who will have all men to be saved, and t
unto the knowledge of the truth" (1 Tim. 2

It is God's will that men be saved. If yo
stumbling around in life and tossing up s
periodic prayers to God but have never come
your knees to the foot of the Cross and r
Jesus Christ, then you are not even in the b
ginning of God's will. God has no reason t
reveal to you anything particular about your lif
because you have not met qualification number
one: Salvation.

God Leads His Own

A well-known New York restaurant and night-
club owner made this statement in a news in-
terview: "I wouldn't be where I am today if it
weren't for the Big Man upstairs."

Of course, that is a true statement in the
sense that the Apostle Paul meant when he told
the pagan Athenians that it is "in Him we live,
and move, and have our being" (Acts 17:28).
Christ is the sustainer of the entire universe,
and nobody would be where he is today without Him.

But as to God personally leading those wh
have not received Jesus Christ as personal Sav
iour, there is not a line of Scripture to indica
that this ordinarily happens. Instead we rea
"And when He putteth forth His own sheep, I
goeth before them, and the sheep follow H
for they know His voice" (John 10:4).

The Apostle John said, "Love not the world, neither the things that are in the world. . . . The world passeth away, and the lust thereof, but he that doeth the will of God abideth forever" (1 John 2:15-17). Who is going to abide forever? Those who do the will of God. But who is the only One who can give eternal life? Jesus Christ. The very first step in walking the pathway of God's will, then, is that you be saved.

If you have never committed your life to Jesus Christ, you cannot expect anything at all from God. He owes you nothing. He is not obligated to you in even the slightest sense.

People reject this. The doctrine of salvation is unpopular because it includes the recognition of sin. Nobody likes to admit sin. And many people resist the idea that they need to be saved.

Confrontation at UCLA

I will never forget sharing in an evangelism blitz with Campus Crusade for Christ on the UCLA campus. About 2,000 kids went person-to-person sharing Christ. UCLA is a stronghold of Judaism—Orthodox, Conservative, and Reformed. It is also known for its Communist groups. UCLA is thus not exactly the most open place to the Gospel, but away we went, sharing Christ. Soon a front page article appeared in the *Daily Bruin* with a cartoon showing a bruin (UCLA's bear mascot) and a Christian standing with his heel on the bruin's neck. Included in the issue was an article written by the dean warning all those on campus talking about Jesus Christ to immediately cease or the administration would take "direct action." The dean cited an article of the constitution of the university which said that the "campus is not to be used for religious conversion."

Talking about sin and salvation is offensive to some people. Who wants to hear about sin? Most people mask it. Sin is not sin. Oh, no. Sin is "a prenatal predilection," psychologists tell us. Sin is an "idiosyncrasy of individuality." Sin is "poor secretion of the endocrine glands"!

But God's will is that people be saved! And basic to salvation is the recognition of sin. This lays it right at your feet. Either you are not saved from your sin and you need to come to Christ because that is God's will, or you are saved and need to reach others with the message of salvation. There is a world out there that needs Jesus Christ. God wants them to be saved, and you and I are the vehicles for the transportation of the Gospel. That is God's will.

You say you do not know what God's will is, but I'll tell you what it is. First, that you know Christ and then that your neighbors hear about Christ. That is His will. So often we sit around twiddling our thumbs, dreaming about God's will in some far distant future when we are not even willing to stand up on our own two feet, walk down the street, and do God's will right now.

God so desired that men be saved that He gave the One whom He loved most, His Son, and sent Him to die on a cross. That is the measure of His love, and that indicates how much He wills that men be saved!

3

The Fizzie Principle

As believers—people in God's family—if we do not know God's will, what are we? Uninformed? No. Searching? No. We are stupid.

"That's pretty rough," you say. "The Bible doesn't talk like that."

Oh? Try this. "Wherefore be ye not unwise, but understanding what the will of the Lord is" (Eph. 5:17). Can you think of another word for unwise? I'll give you a hint; it starts with "s."

OK, maybe stupid is a little stronger, a bit more vivid. But it's certainly the same idea.

Furthermore, the preceding verse tells us we have to get on with it; we don't have much time. We are to be "redeeming the time, because the days are evil" (v. 16).

You say, "But I am looking for God's will. Maybe I am stupid, but can I help that?"

Yes, you can help it. If you had no choice but to be stupid about God's will, the Bible would not command you to be "not unwise." The way to be not unwise is covered in the very next verse. "Be not drunk with wine, wherein is excess; but be filled with the Spirit" (v. 18).

First, if you want to know God's will, you must be saved. Second, you must be Spirit-filled. That is the teaching of the Word of God.

Many Christians say, "I don't understand why God hasn't revealed whom I am to marry?" Others say, "Why doesn't He show me what job I should take, what business deal I should enter into, what I ought to purchase, whether I ought to move to another home, or what I ought to do about some specific problem? Why doesn't God do something for me and show me His will?" And all the time these people are not even Spirit-filled, which is clearly revealed as His will. Why should God show a person something if he is not even fulfilling that which God has already clearly stated as His will?

What does it mean to be Spirit-filled? Let me give you a short theology lesson. We will call it theology of the Spirit-filled life. When you were saved, the moment you received Jesus Christ, the Holy Spirit came to live within you. There is no Christian who does not possess the

Holy Spirit. "If any man have not the Spirit of Christ, he is none of His" (Rom. 8:9 cf. 1 Cor. 6:19; 12:12-13). Yet it is amazing how many Christians think they do not have the Holy Spirit.

I have sat in church and heard sincere people pray, "O, God, send Your Spirit," and have thought to myself, *No, He is here. He is here!* I have heard people pray, "God give me more of Your Spirit," as if He came in doses.

The Holy Spirit is a person; He lives within you. "Know ye not that your body is the temple of the Holy Ghost?" (1 Cor. 6:19) So many times we ask for what we already have! We pray for the Holy Spirit, and He is already here.

Have you ever analyzed your prayers?

You pray, "God, give me more love for so-and-so." The Bible says the "love of God is shed abroad in our hearts" (Rom. 5:5).

You say, "God, I need more grace." God says that the grace He has already given you is sufficient (2 Cor. 12:9).

You cry, "O Lord, I need more strength." The Bible says you "can do all things through Christ" who strengthens you (Phil. 4:13).

"O God, guide me," you say. And He is thinking, "I'm trying. Why don't you follow?"

"God, I need power," you cry. In fact, you have had power since the Holy Spirit came upon you (Acts 1:8).

Complete in Him

When will Christians realize that they have everything? Peter wrote, "According as His divine power hath given unto us all things that pertain unto life and godliness" (2 Peter 1:3). You do not lack anything! But so many emaciated Christians go around and say, "Well, I just don't have the power to do this or that."

The Apostle Paul said to the Colossians, "And ye are complete in Him" (Col. 2:10). Complete! What are you looking for? What are you asking for? James told you what to ask for—"wisdom" (James 1:5)—and that is the sense to know what you already have and not ask for it! By the same token, we do not need to ask for the Spirit; He is in us already.

Since we have the Spirit, we also have power, for Jesus said, "But you shall receive power when the Holy Spirit has come upon you" (Acts 1:8, NASB). The word for power in the Greek is *dunamis,* from which we got our word "dynamite." You are literally walking dynamite.

You may say, "Oh, yeah? I'm not sure; I think I'm a dud. I not only don't explode; I don't even fizzle too loudly."

But you are dynamite. The power is all there. What is so often not there is the release of that power. It is one thing to possess the Spirit; it is something else to be filled with the Spirit.

A Fizzie is a small tablet used to make a

soft drink; it's sort of a flavored Alka-Seltzer. Put it in a glass of water and its flavor is released throughout the water. This concentrated, compact power pill is no good as long as it sits on the bottom of the glass. It has to release its energy to fill the glass, and then it turns the water into something new. If it is a grape Fizzie, you get a glass of grape drink. The flavor of the tablet determines the flavor of the water.

In a measure, that pictures how the Spirit of God operates in a human life. He is in the Christian all the time as a compact, concentrated, powerful force of divine energy. The question is, has He ever been able to release that power, to fill your life so that you can become what He is? A Christian not yielded to the Spirit of God does not manifest the Christ-life. The Spirit of God has to permeate a life if that life is to radiate Him.

We cannot do anything apart from being filled with the Spirit.

I have a glove. If I say to the glove, "Play the piano," what does the glove do? Nothing. The glove cannot play the piano. But if I put my hand in the glove and play the piano, what happens? Music! If I put my hand in a glove, the glove moves. The glove does not get pious and say, "Oh, hand, show me the way to go." It does not say anything; it just goes. Spirit-filled people do not stumble and mumble around trying to find out what God wants. They just go!

People often ask, "How do I know my spiritual gift?" The best way is to live a Spirit-filled life, see what God does through you, look back in retrospect and say, "Oh, that's what I do when God has control of me. Apparently, that is my gift." There is no need to get analytical. The whole point is that we need the Spirit of God to be released in our lives. This is simply a matter of decisions. When you get up in the morning, you decide what you are going to wear. Next you decide what you are going to eat for breakfast. And so it goes through the day— one decision after another. The Spirit-filled life is yielding every decision to the control of the Spirit.

Peter's Experience

An illustration comes from the life of the Apostle Peter. When Peter was near Jesus Christ, he had amazing power. Thus he loved to be where Jesus was. On one occasion the disciples were out on the Sea of Galilee (Matt. 14:22-33). The boat was tossing in a storm and they couldn't get to Capernaum. (The winds very often turn the Sea of Galilee into a swirl, keeping a boat moving in a circle.)

Suddenly one of the men in the boat looked out and said, "Someone is walking on the water!"

Sure enough, with robes flowing in the wind, here came Jesus walking across the whitecaps.

Peter cried out, "Is that You, Lord?"

The Lord answered, "It is I."

Peter said, "Can I come?"

You may wonder why Peter said that. Why didn't he wait in the boat till Jesus got there? But that wouldn't have been like Peter. He said to himself, "Jesus is over there. I am over here. That is not good. I must go over there." It never entered his mind that normally he was not able to walk on water. That was not even a problem. When he saw Jesus, he had such a desire to be with Him that he went.

But when Peter got out on those tossing waves, he looked down and thought, "What am I doing here?" He began to sink, but the Lord lifted him back up.

The point is that when he was near Jesus, Peter could do the miraculous. He and Jesus walked back together on the water.

Some time later, Jesus was talking to His disciples and asked, "Who do men say that I am?"

They answered, "Oh, some people think You are Jeremiah; some people think You are Elijah; some people think You are one of the prophets."

He said, "Who do you think I am?"

Peter responded, "Thou art the Christ, the Son of the living God" (Matt. 16:16). Then, I feel sure, he wondered, Where did that come from?

Jesus said, "Flesh and blood did not reveal this to you, Peter, but My Father in heaven did" (see Matt. 16:13-17).

Peter probably said, "I thought so. I surely didn't know that." You see, when Peter was near Jesus, he not only did the miraculous, he said the miraculous. Is it any wonder he wanted to be near Him?

When he was near Christ, Peter had miraculous courage. He was in the Garden of Gethsemane when a whole band of soldiers—as many as 500—came to arrest Jesus. They came marching in with all their regalia. In front of them came the chief priests, and before the chief priests came the servants of the priests. Peter was standing with the Lord. Maybe his thoughts went something like this: "They think they are going to take Jesus away. No, they won't!"

Since Peter did not ever want to be removed from the presence of Jesus, he took out a sword. He started with the first guy in line, who happened to be Malchus, the servant of the high priest. The Bible says Peter cut off Malchus' ear, but if I know Peter, he was going for his head. Peter was ready to take on the whole Roman army. You see, when he was with Jesus, he had miraculous courage.

A little while later, Jesus went in to be tried, and Peter stood outside. He was removed from Jesus. What happened then to this powerful man—this man who could walk on water, speak with divine inspiration, exhibit miraculous courage? When he got separated from Jesus, he was a failure. On three occasions he denied Christ. Apart from Jesus, he was nothing.

Ready for Burial?

But the day came that Jesus was to ascend into heaven. You say, "Oh, no. If Peter is a coward when he is 100 feet away from Jesus, what are we going to do with him when Jesus goes away into heaven? We might as well bury him. He's worthless!"

Yet, a short time after Christ's ascension, Peter stands before the enemies of Christ and says, "Ye men of Judea, and all ye that dwell at Jerusalem, be this known unto you, and hearken to my words" (Acts 2:14). Wham! He takes a text from Joel and away he goes. He says they have killed the Prince of Life, desired a murderer to be released to them, and denied the Holy One. Then he proceeds to proclaim Christ fearlessly, firing the Gospel out with both barrels. Where did Peter get such courage?

The next time we read about Peter is in Acts 3. He and John went into the Temple through the Gate Beautiful, where there was a man who had been lame for 40 years. Peter said to him, "Look at us!" The man looked, and Peter said, "Silver and gold have I none, but such as I have give I thee: In the name of Jesus Christ of Nazareth rise up and walk" (Acts 3:6). The lame man stood up and started leaping and jumping and praising God. Peter had not only said the miraculous, he had done it too.

In the next chapter of Acts, Peter is persecuted. He exhibits a boldness that is remarkable, the same courage he displayed in the garden. You might say to yourself, "I don't understand this. Peter had these traits only when Jesus was near. Yet, with Jesus gone back to heaven, Peter displays these same great traits again. What is going on?" Acts 2:4 gives us the secret. Before Peter ever did any exploits, he was one of those who "were filled with the Holy [Ghost]" (Acts 2:4).

Let me draw a conclusion. When Peter was filled with the Holy Spirit, he had the same power as when he was standing next to Jesus Christ! Now here's something exciting! Do you know what the Spirit-filled life is? It is living every moment as though you are standing in the presence of Jesus Christ! Not too complicated, is it? Someone might think I am confusing the issue because the Holy Spirit and Christ are different. But by what name does Paul call the Holy Spirit? "The Spirit of Christ" (Rom. 8:9).

Jesus said that when He went away, He would send *allos,* "another" Comforter (John 14:16). There are two words in the Greek for another: *heteros* and *allos. Heteros* means another of a different kind, and *allos* means another of exactly the same kind!

Here is my Bible. If I said to you, "Give me *heteros biblos,*" you could give me any book. If I said to you, "Give me *allos biblos,*" you would have to give another Bible exactly like mine, with all my markings and cuts and cracks. This is *allos.* When Jesus said, "I am going to send you another comforter," He said *allos,* another exactly like Me. The Spirit-filled life is nothing more than living in the conscious presence of the indwelling Christ.

We tend to get so fogged up about the Spirit-filled life. Paul says we are simply to be filled with the Spirit rather than being drunk. We are to be under the control of the Spirit rather than under the influence of wine (Eph. 5:18).

How does the Spirit-filled life express itself? "In psalms and hymns and spiritual songs, singing and making melody in your heart to the Lord; giving thanks always for all things unto God and the Father in the name of our Lord Jesus Christ" (Eph. 5:19-20). Then Paul goes all the way down the line, describing the life-style of Spirit-filled people. Wives will submit, husbands will love their wives, fathers will not provoke their children to wrath, children will obey, servants will work well, and masters will be fair. This is how Spirit-filled people are to live (Eph. 5:22—6:9).

Filled with the Word

The curious thing is that Colossians 3 has the same list: submission, speaking in psalms and spiritual songs, wives submitting, husbands loving, children obeying, parents not provoking, servants, masters. Only here Paul does not link such living to the filling of the Spirit. He says it is the result of letting "the Word of Christ dwell in you richly in all wisdom" (Col. 3:16).

Do you see what the Spirit-filled life is? It is being saturated with the things of Christ, with His Word, His Person.

You might say, "Well, you know, I'd like that. I'd like to be saturated with Christ. How do I do that?"

The only way is to study the Book that discloses all He is!

You say, "I tried reading the Bible, but I didn't get anything."

Let me share how I study the Bible, and how the Bible has come alive to me. I began in 1 John. One day I sat down and read all five chapters straight through. It took me 20 minutes. Reading one book straight through was terrific. (The books of the Bible weren't written as an assortment of good little individual verses. They were written with flow and context.)

The next day, I sat down and read 1 John straight through again. The third day, I sat down and read 1 John straight through. The fourth day, straight through again. The fifth day, I sat down and read it again. I did this for 30 days. Do you know what happened at the end of 30 days? I knew what was in 1 John.

Someone says to you, "Where in the Bible does it talk about confessing our sins?" You see a mental image of 1 John, first chapter, right-hand column, half-way down (depending on your Bible). "Where does it say to love not the world?" Second chapter, right-hand column, half-way down. Where does it talk about sin unto death? Chapter 5, last page. You know 1 John!

Next, I went to the Gospel of John. I divided the Gospel of John into three sections of seven chapters each. I read the first seven chapters for 30 days, the next seven for the next 30 days, and the last seven for 30 days. In 90 days, I had read the entire Gospel of John 30 times. Where does it talk about the Good Shepherd? Chapter 10, right-hand column, starts in the middle, goes down, flip the page, go on down.

Where does it talk about the vine and the branches? Chapter 15. Where does it talk about

Jesus' friends? Chapter 15, over in the next column and a little farther down. Where does it talk about Jesus' arrest in the garden? John 18. The restoration of Peter? John 21. The woman at the well? John 4. The Bread of Life? John 6. Nicodemus? John 3. The wedding at Cana? John 2.

You might say, "My, are you smart!" No, I am not smart. I read it 30 times. Even I can get it then! Isaiah said to learn "precept upon precept, line upon line, . . . here a little, and there a little" (see Isa. 28:10-13). Then you have hidden it in your heart. After a while you are no longer a concordance cripple!

Planned Neglect

The more you study the Word of God, the more it saturates your mind and life. Someone is reported to have asked a concert violinist in New York's Carnegie Hall how she became so skilled. She said that it was by "planned neglect." She planned to neglect everything that was not related to her goal.

Some less important things in your life could stand some planned neglect so that you might give yourself to studying the Word of God. Do you know what would happen? The more you would study the Word of God, the more your mind would be saturated with it. It will be no problem then for you to think of Christ. You won't be able to stop thinking of Him.

To be Spirit-filled is to live a Christ-conscious life, and there is no shortcut to that. You can't go and get yourself super-dedicated to live a Christ-conscious life. The only way you can be saturated with the thoughts of Christ is to saturate yourself with the Book that is all about Him. And this is God's will, that you not only be saved but that you also be Spirit-filled.

4

The Priority of Purity

To some people who have been looking for the will of God for a long time, this is going to seem quite obvious. "For this is the will of God, even your sanctification" (1 Thes. 4:3-7). God desires every believer to be sanctified. What does "sanctified" mean? Let's use the word pure instead. Paul is talking in this passage about practical purity and he gives four principles.

Abstain from Fornication

Stay away from sexual sin. It does not say to avoid sex; it says to stay away from sexual sin. Of course, this means we must not get involved in sexual acts that are wrong. It also means we should stay clear away from those things. Some

Christians who wouldn't dream of doing those things sit and watch somebody else doing them or read about them in some book and call this entertainment. We should have no part in those things.

I am not a prude; I think sex is a glorious thing. God invented it. If He invented it, it is good. But He designed it for the beauty of the marriage relationship and nowhere else. For a person to think that he can cheat God and get kicks out of sex apart from marriage is to believe the devil's lie.

It is absurd for a young person (or anyone else) who is living in sexual impurity to say, "God, show me Your will." Such a person is not even doing what this text of Scripture says is His will. Why should God disclose some further will?

Stay away from immoral sex. That is a simple principle. Someone inevitably says, "How far away?" Far away enough to be pure. Sanctified. Set apart wholly unto God.

Am I saying that you can't hold hands with the one you love? That is not the issue. Do I mean that you can't kiss? I don't mean that, either. The Bible says, "All things are lawful unto me, but all things are not expedient. All things are lawful for me, but I will not be brought under the power of any" (1 Cor. 6:12). You can be blessed by God only so long as you are controlling what you do for His honor. When lust controls you, you have crossed the line. It's a simple principle.

Control Your Body

The second principle concerning practical purity is expressed in 1 Thessalonians 4:4. "Every one of you should know how to possess his vessel in sanctification and honor." In the Greek, there are two possible meanings of this word *vessel*: "wife" or "body." In the context, I take it to mean "body." What Paul is saying is that we are to control our bodies. That is purity.

We ought to keep our bodies in subjection to insure that we are honoring God. That includes controlling the way we dress and the things we do with our bodies. This principle covers the whole area of the lust of the flesh, and not just sexual things. A person can dishonor God by overdressing to attract attention to oneself. Gluttony also puts one in the position of dishonoring God and committing sin because it is obvious to everyone that the glutton cannot control the desire to eat. Nothing which gratifies the body to the dishonoring of God can have a place in the will of God.

Subdue Your Passions

The Christian is not to live "in the lust of concupiscence (evil desire which has to do with

sexual things) even as the Gentiles (heathen)
which know not God" (1 Thes. 4:5). What is
Paul saying? Don't act like the rest of the world
acts—they are guided by their passions.

A young lady of 16 came up to me one time
with tears streaming down her cheeks. She said
to me, "John, I can't take any more," she said.
"I am going to kill myself." I asked her why,
and she replied, "I have been involved with so
many boys since I was 13 years old that I can't
look at myself in the mirror." We sat down and
talked about God's love and complete forgive-
ness. That teenager invited Jesus into her life.
Later her eyes sparkled through the tears as she
said, "You know something? I feel forgiven." I
assured her that she was. She went out from
that place no longer to live in the gutter but to
set her affections on things above.

One of the great, liberating things about
Christianity is that it takes you out of the gutter
and lifts you up. Stay up! Don't act like the
godless.

Treat Others Fairly

No man is to "go beyond and defraud his brother
in any matter" (I Thes. 4:6). In other words,
don't take advantage of people.

Some people step on others' necks to get what
they want. Some people use others in a sexual
way to gratify their own desires. Others use

people in a business way. There are many ways to use others. Don't do it for "the Lord is the avenger of all such."

You may say, "I don't like those rules. God is narrow-minded." Then verse 8 is for you. "He therefore that despiseth, despiseth not man, but God, who hath also given unto us His Holy Spirit." If you mistreat people, you really mistreat and despise God.

In verse 7, Paul sums up what we have been saying. "For God hath not called us unto uncleanness, but unto holiness." God's calling—God's will—is that we be sanctified, holy, pure.

Robert Murray McCheyne spoke at the ordination of young Dan Edwards in the 1860s. He said something like this: "Mr. Edwards, . . . do not forget the inner man, the heart. The cavalry officer knows that his life depends upon his saber, so he keeps it clean. Every stain he wipes off with the greatest care. Mr. Edwards, you are God's chosen instrument. According to your purity, so shall be your success. It is not great talent; it is not great ideas that God uses; it is great likeness to Jesus Christ. Mr. Edwards, a holy man is an awesome weapon in the hand of God" (see 2 Tim. 2:21). McCheyne was right, and God's will is that you be holy—sanctified.

5

Silencing the Critics

Picture a young man who is very earnestly wanting to know God's will for his life's work. He's so dedicated to God that he's even willing to be a missionary, which seems to be the ultimate sacrifice in the eyes of some people.

But our young friend, despite his dedication, has some problems. He is a little headstrong. He seems to have trouble getting along with those in authority over him. His reasons for rebellion are very good, of course, at least in his eyes.

Finally, our young seeker-after-God's will takes his problem to a wise old pastor. "I believe God wants me to be a missionary," he says, "but I'm not sure whether He wants me to be a home missionary or a foreign missionary."

The pastor looks him straight in the eye. "Young man," he says, "what you need to be first of all is a 'submissionary.' You need to learn what submission means."

Hard words? Perhaps. But true. The Apostle Peter wrote, "Submit yourselves to every ordinance of man for the Lord's sake: whether it be to the king as supreme, or unto governors, as unto them that are sent by him for the punishment of evildoers, and for the praise of them that do well. For so is the will of God" (1 Peter 2:13-15).

What is it God wills that you do? Submit. What kind of submission is He talking about? Scripture outlines several kinds, including to parents and other believers. But here Peter calls specifically for the kind of submission that makes you the best possible citizen in the society in which you live.

Who is it that we are trying to reach? The world. If we are not the epitome of what a citizen should be in the world, we will certainly harm our testimonies. God not only commands our submission to those in authority, but He clearly tells us the reason. "For so is the will of God, that with well doing ye may put to silence the ignorance of foolish men" (1 Peter 2:15).

Do you know what the critics of Christ look for in Christians? Faults! How are we going to prevent them from finding faults? Eliminate the faults. We need to put to silence the ignorance of foolish men.

How are you going to silence your critics? By living an exemplary life within society. That is Peter's point. The Christian is not a revolutionary. If there is a lawful way to make needed change, he takes that route. He works. He strives to be the best man he can be and to make the best contribution to society he can make, but he does it within the law.

Don't ever abuse your freedom. Do not use your freedom as a cloak for being malicious and evil (1 Peter 2:16).

Someone will inevitably say, "I don't believe in this restriction. God has told me in my heart that it is wrong. So, I am going to break this law or resist that rule."

Wait a minute! The Bible says not to hide your maliciousness under the blanket of so-called Christian liberty. God says, "Honor all men. Love the brotherhood. Fear God. Honor the king" (1 Peter 2:17).

If you happen to be employed by somebody, be "subject to your masters with all fear" (2:18). You may say, "You don't understand my boss!" The Scripture continues, ". . . not only to the good and gentle, but also to the froward." The word *froward* means "perverse." Do you have a perverse boss? What are you supposed to do? Submit, lovingly and willfully.

Shake the World

So many times I think to myself that if Christians ever learned to live the kind of life Peter described we would knock the world right off its pins. But sometimes the world can't distinguish us from itself. The Apostle Paul calls us who are Christians working for non-Christian employers to give them an honest day's work for a day's pay and show them that is the norm for a Christian (see Eph. 6:5-8).

If you are the citizen of a certain state, obey the laws of that state so that people might know that your faith is real, that it reaches and influences every area of your life. I always get disturbed if a guy who has a Christian slogan on his bumper weaves in and out of traffic like a maniac.

The principle of good citizenship is further upheld by Paul, who says that when the church chooses an elder, it is to pick one who is blameless (see 1 Tim. 3:10).

You may ask, "Am I supposed to obey every law in the land?" Yes, every law. If you do not agree wtih them, that doesn't change the matter. Obey them. Now if you know a way to work politically to change poor laws, fine; but until they are changed, obey them.

But what if they tell you to do something that violates God's clear revelation and command? Then do *not* obey them! That is the only exception. This is what happened when the Jewish rulers took Peter and John into custody. They told them not to preach any more in the name of Jesus. But Peter and John answered, "You judge whether we ought to obey God or men." And they went right out of that place and started preaching (see Acts 4:18-20). The only time a believer is ever to violate the law of the land is when the law either forbids him to do what he has been told to do by direct command from God or commands him to do what God forbids.

What am I saying? It is that God wants us to be the kind of citizens in the world who will draw the attention of the world. We need to be different. We need to have the qualities of salt and light (Matt. 5:13-16). That involves submission, which is clearly commanded in the Scripture.

6

Facing the Flak

Many would-be followers of Jesus come to Him with dreams of greatness, which are good in their place. Jesus put down the disciples for arguing about which of them would be greatest, and told them that real greatness centers in being of service to others (Mark 9:33-35). But Jesus also encouraged their aspirations for greatness with such statements as, "Ye which have followed Me . . . shall sit upon 12 thrones, judging the 12 tribes of Israel" (Matt. 19:28).

But in the will of God, greatness follows along behind suffering, often far behind. And if a man signs on with Jesus with greatness in mind, he better be aware that suffering comes first. Otherwise, the will of God may begin to look pretty undesirable to him after he's been on the way a short time.

One fellow came to Jesus claiming he wanted to do the Lord's will. "Lord, I will follow Thee withersoever Thou goest," he declared.

Jesus replied, "Foxes have holes, and birds of the air have nests; but the Son of man hath not where to lay His head" (Luke 9:57-58). He wanted this would-be follower to know that the will of God involves suffering.

The Apostle Peter wrote, "But the God of all grace, who hath called us unto His eternal glory by Christ Jesus, after that ye have suffered a while, make you perfect . . ." (1 Peter 5:10). Suffering is par for the course for Christians.

That is why the Apostle Peter also wrote about "them that suffer according to the will of God" (1 Peter 4:19).

Someone may say, "I should suffer? That part I am qualified for. Boy, do I suffer. I bear a real cross. My parents are my cross." Or, "My husband/wife is my cross." Or, "My mother-in-law is my cross."

But that is not the kind of suffering Peter was talking about. He wrote, "For it is better, if the will of God be so, that ye suffer for well-doing, than for evil-doing" (1 Peter 3:17). We are to suffer, not because we have failed to be the right kind of young person, not because we are antagonistic, grumpy, grouchy, or out of whack somewhere, but we should suffer for doing what is right.

When that happens, Peter said, "Rejoice, inasmuch as ye are partakers of Christ's sufferings" (1 Peter 4:13). You ought to be happy about it. "If ye be reproached for the name of Christ, happy are ye; for the spirit of glory and of God resteth upon you . . . but let none of you suffer as a murderer, or as a thief, or as an evildoer, or as a busybody in other men's matters" (1 Peter 4:14-15).

The passage continues, "Yet if any man suffer as a Christian . . ." (v. 16). Do you understand what he is talking about? Do you see what is par for the course? If you are a Christian who is living a godly life in an ungodly world, you will suffer.

The Apostle Paul puts it, "Yea, and all that will live godly in Christ Jesus shall suffer persecution" (2 Tim. 3:12).

You may say, "But I don't suffer any persecution." Then maybe you're not living a godly life in the face of the world. But if you do suffer, it is a wonderful thing. The Spirit of grace and glory rests on you (1 Peter 4:14).

Evangelism isn't just the preacher's job. It is yours. Nor is it completed simply by distributing tracts everywhere, however good that may be. Evangelism involves living a godly life in the face of an ungodly world. And that will bring persecution, because the world does not like Jesus.

Out in the Bushes?

Consider the words of Paul as recorded in Philippians 1:29: "For unto you it is given in the behalf of Christ, not only to believe on Him, but also to suffer for His sake." Here is something shocking. Suffering is linked with faith. The Bible never sees a Christian at any time who doesn't suffer—because anybody who lives a godly life in the world will get the flak that the world throws back. If you are waltzing through life comfortably, it either means that you are not living a godly life or you are living it out in the bushes somewhere where the ungodly world cannot see it.

The Bible shows how we can live a godly life in an ungodly world with success. Acts 4 records how Peter once unloaded a bombshell sermon on the leaders of Israel. He blistered them so many times that I am surprised they did not stone him on the spot. When he finished preaching, the Bible says the Jews "laid hands" on Peter and John (v. 3). It was not to ordain them, we can be sure! It was to put them in custody. But the result of Peter's sermon was that many believed. The number of men converted came to 5,000.

And there were probably another 5,000

women and children. By the time the church was a few weeks old, they had won perhaps 20,000 people. In the next chapter we hear about their multiplying, but it doesn't tell us how many because they were beyond counting!

But let's get back to Peter and John, who were thrown in jail for the night. In the morning they were taken out, and they were asked, "By what power, or by what name, have ye done this?" (v. 7)

I imagine Peter thought, "What a question! Does that guy know what he is saying? I get to answer that!"

In a way, Satan is foolish. He overreaches himself. He thought, "I'll fix them. I'll get them captured." Do you know what happened? They were slapped in front of the Sanhedrin (the top leaders of Israel) and they preached Jesus to the Sanhedrin, an opportunity they never would have had unless Satan had arranged it. Satan does that all the time. He put Paul in the Philippian jail, and the jailer and his whole family were saved. He put Jesus on a cross, and what happened? Jesus redeemed the world. Satan doesn't really know what he's getting into. And God is sovereign.

Peter and John got into this thing, and they just took their suffering. They didn't hassle. There was no fighting, running, hiding behind a portico, or any of that sort of thing. They moved ahead in confidence that this was God's opportunity.

Then Peter, filled with the Holy Spirit (v. 8), preached the name of Jesus Christ and closed with an invitation in classic evangelistic style. "Neither is there salvation in any other; for there is none other name under heaven given among men, whereby we must be saved" (v. 12).

Not Out of Order

Picture Peter standing in the hall of hewn stone near the temple. The whole Sanhedrin is sitting there, including Caiaphas who is sitting behind them in the high priest's chair. Peter is preaching Jesus! And he is not out of order. They had asked him by what name he healed that lame man by the Gate Beautiful, and he is only answering them honestly.

Then the suffering got worse.

The authorities commanded Peter and John not to speak at all nor teach in the name of Jesus (v. 18). Peter and John answered, "Whether it be right in the sight of God to hearken unto you more than unto God, judge ye" (v. 19). That was a question the Sanhedrin had a hard time answering because they fancied themselves religious and said they believed in God. If they said, "You ought to obey us instead of God," it would plainly put them at odds with God. If they said, "You ought to obey God, not us," that would also put them at odds with God, and exonerate the disciples. Peter had stumped them.

The authorities gave Peter and John a lecture and further threatened them. They couldn't figure out any way to punish them because they were afraid of the people, so they let them go.

Peter and John ran back to the assembly of Christians, and they all had a glorious time praising God. Then they prayed. They did not say, "God, protect us; they are after us."

They prayed, "Lord, behold their threatenings; and grant unto Thy servants, that with all boldness they may speak Thy Word" (v. 29).

They did not say, "Help us." They said, "Empower us and send us back again!"

"And when they had prayed, the place was shaken where they were assembled together; and they were all filled with the Holy Ghost, and they spake the word of God with boldness" (v. 31).

What does the next verse say? "And the multitude of them that believed . . ." (v. 32). They had results! They went out and turned that town upside down.

It was a beautiful thing, you see, because they submitted themselves to suffering. They confronted their world boldly; they did not back down. They did not sneak out or get into "Gospel blimp" tactics. They were not trying to slip the Gospel into somebody's hip pocket. They confronted the world head-on with the claims of Christ, in love, and they let the chips fly. Do you know what happened? They got opportunities they could never have had otherwise, and God gave them more boldness than ever.

One of the problems of evangelism today is that Christians are not willing to stand nose-to-nose with the world and tell it like it is concerning Jesus Christ. The Gospel is emasculated to accommodate everybody's prejudice. We need boldness. It is sad that the boldness of Peter and John is far from what most of us experience in our lives. I pray God that He will give us more boldness.

Confronting the Militants

On one occasion, I was invited to speak at a particular college, with 15,000 to 20,000 students in a predominantly Jewish area of Los Angeles. I was asked to speak on the philosophical basis for Christianity. Many students were there, and the Jewish radical faction was there also. Some were militantly anti-Christian. There they were, all ready to listen to what I had to say.

Sometimes when you preach you just feel the power of God going through you. It is as though you are standing there but God is doing everything. God gave me clear thinking and a fluid voice. The auditorium was dead quiet, and I was ready for tomatoes and eggs. For one hour, I developed the philosophical basis for Christianity. The last 10 minutes I spent proving that Jesus is the Messiah.

When I was done, the militant organization demanded that I be banned from the campus permanently. I began to get obscene letters in the mail, and threats against my life and family. They were also going to come on a Sunday morning and blow up my church. I began to get obscene and threatening telephone calls at 2 and 3 o'clock in the morning.

For the second time in my life I began to realize what it is to confront the world and to find the hostility that is meant for Jesus coming to me. I cannot say that I have ever had a more exhilarating or thrilling experience than in those days. (And they are still going on.) I confronted the world with boldness in the power of the Spirit of God, and things happened!

I could have stayed away from that campus that day for fear that it would wipe out my ministry or endanger my life. But I went. A student came up to me after that meeting, while we were still there and the rumbles were still going on, and said to me, "Could I come and talk with you?"

A week after our talk, he came to my office, sat down, and said, "What you said made sense, and I want to know Jesus Christ." He is a brother in Christ now, and his salvation was an outcome of my going into that inferno. And he has already reproduced himself by leading others to Christ.

You may say, "MacArthur, you did not have to get yourself in hot water."

Oh, yes, I did. I am expendable for the sake of one young man! If God wanted me even to lose my life, I should willingly lose it for His sake. That was Paul's attitude. Paul said that he gloried in infirmity, tribulation, necessity, even in persecution, because when he was persecuted, people got saved, and that is good.

A Christian is expendable. You may not get physical flak but may suffer intellectual persecution instead. You may be quietly ostracized from society. You may be politely shunned at the water cooler. People may take a "there-goes-the-weirdo" attitude. And that causes a deflated ego problem. Every person wants so much to be accepted. But you cannot be accepted by the world and be effective for the Lord.

I am not a masochist. I take no pleasure in being abused, spiritually or otherwise, and I am not talking about going around saying, "Oh, poor me. I am persecuted. Aren't I spiritual?" God help us, no. But I am talking about a willingness to be bold, a willingness to face the world and let the chips fly. Don't ever water down the Gospel. If the truth offends, then let it offend. People have been living their whole lives in offense to God; let them be offended for a while.

Consider Paul's words in his letter to the Philippians: Yea, and if I be offered upon the sacrifice and service of your faith, I joy, and rejoice with you all" (2:17). What did Paul mean? If I have to die as a sacrifice for you to be saved, that is good. If I have to offer my life as a sacrifice for your joy, I love it.

In his letter to the Colossians, Paul rejoiced about his suffering. You may think Paul was out of his mind. No. He said "[I] rejoice in my sufferings for you, and fill up that which is behind of the afflictions of Christ in my flesh" (1:24). What does he mean? The world would like to get at Jesus. They do not persecute Christians because they dislike them; they persecute Christians because they dislike Jesus. They can't get at Him because He is in heaven, so they get at you and me.

Paul said that he was enduring the suffering that was meant for Jesus; he was filling up in his body the afflictions of Jesus. The world is not done killing Jesus. Paul stood in the world's way so that he would get to die for the One who had died for him. In the same way, we should count it a joy to stand and take the arrows meant for Jesus.

Paul said, "I bear in my body the marks of the Lord Jesus" (Gal. 6:17). These scars over here—these were not for me. They were for Jesus, but I took them for Him! Are you willing to suffer for Him who suffered for you? Are you willing to confront the world? That is the will of God.

7

You're It

God's will is that you be saved, Spirit-filled, sanctified, submissive, and suffering. God's Word makes all this clear. Do not read on until you have grasped these five principles.

You say, "MacArthur, you were going to tell me what school I should go to. You were going to tell me God's will, specifically. You haven't done it!"

OK, let me give you the final principle, but hold onto your seat! You may want to jump up and shout! If you are doing all five of the basic things, do you know what the next principle of God's will is? Do whatever you want! If those five elements of God's will are operating in your life, who is running your wants? God is! The

Psalmist said, "Delight thyself also in the Lord; and He shall give thee the desires of thine heart" (Ps. 37:4). God does not say He will fulfill all the desires that are there. He says He will put the desires there! If you are living a godly life, He will give you the right desires.

People say to me, "Why did you go into your present ministry when you had such an enjoyable ministry before in another area?"

I always answer, "Because I wanted to."

"Aha. Self-will."

It is not self-will. It is God's will.

I had a friend come to me and say, "John, I don't know where the Lord wants me to serve."

I said to him, "Marty, if you had your choice of any service in the world, what would you want?"

He said, "Oh, I have such a burden for my people Israel. I speak French fluently, and Paris is just loaded with Jewish people who don't know Jesus. I personally would like to go to Paris as a missionary to the Jews."

I checked him on the five spiritual principles and said, "Marty, have you done all these things?"

He replied, "Yes, I honestly believe that I am committed to Christ in these areas."

I said, "Marty, good-bye, have a nice trip."

He hesitated and said, "But I have to write to 42 mission boards."

I said, "No! Go."

He said, "But it is only my desire."

"Then trust that it is God who planted it. Get out of here."

He joined a faith mission and signed up for France. We put up a big plaque in our church: "Marty Wolfe goes to France." He raised all of his support and today he is serving Christ—in Canada!

What happened? Once he was the right guy, it was no big problem where he went. He is in the city of Montreal, working with French-speaking Jews. He had the right idea; God had a different city.

This brings up another crucial principle. Imagine trying to steer and change the direction of a stationary tractor-truck. Tough assignment. It would take huge cranes and chains to even budge it. But once rolling, a truck weighing 36,000 pounds is not difficult to control.

Once Marty was rolling, God took over the steering wheel with the strong arms of His will and it was easy. I suppose God could have hauled in His celestial crane, picked up and pushed Marty in the right direction, but He likes to use people who are already moving.

Listen to this commentary on one of the greatest of the Apostles: "And it came to pass, as Peter passed throughout all [areas], he came down also to the saints who dwelt at Lydda.

And there he found a certain man named Aeneas, which had kept his bed eight years, and was sick of the palsy. And Peter said unto him, 'Aeneas, Jesus Christ maketh thee whole: arise, and make thy bed.' And he arose immediately. And all that dwelt at Lydda and Sharon saw him, and turned to the Lord" (Acts 9:32-35).

This thrilling account records that God used Peter to heal a sick man and start a revival. What a blessed experience of serving in the Lord's will! And neatly tucked into this event is a simple little thought, "As Peter passed throughout all areas."

Peter was already on the move, available for open doors. That's when God directed him to Lydda. Remember, God has His richest ministries for His busiest saints.

We find in Genesis a fascinating illustration of the same truth: "And he said, 'Blessed be the Lord God of my master Abraham, who hath not left destitute my master of His mercy and His truth: I being in the way, the Lord led me to the house of my master's brethren'" (Gen. 24:27). The servant was sent by Abraham to find a wife for Isaac. He didn't even know who or what he was looking for. But he was involved in service and the Lord took it from there.

Get into the mainstream of what God is doing and let Him lead you to that perfect will.

On his second missionary journey Paul fulfilled the ministry God had planned for Galatia, a large province in the Roman Empire. He successfully strengthened, encouraged, and confirmed the saints. The job, for the present, was done. But Paul was not done, he was moving. He was a pattern of persistence.

Paul headed west, not knowing God's will specifically, but rolling so God could steer him. The next province was Asia Minor with its cities of Ephesus, Smyrna, Philadelphia, Laodicea, Colosse, Sardis, Pergamos, and Thyatira. Paul moved with Silas and Timothy toward Asia Minor, thrilled with the prospect of bringing people there the Gospel.

Suddenly, like a concrete wall on a highway, they were forbidden by the Holy Spirit to preach the Gospel in Asia (Acts 16:6). We don't know how God stopped them, but He did. The closed door changed their direction and they went north to Mysia, hoping to enter the province of Bithynia. "But the Spirit suffered them not" (16:7). Another roadblock. They had been stopped from going north and south and toward Galatia to the east. What now? At this point, we might have said, "All doors are closed, we may as well go home." But Paul didn't say that. There was still the west! So they followed the borderline between Asia Minor and Bithynia leading west until they came to the Aegean Sea. They were at the beach town of Troas, "and a vision appeared to Paul in the night. There stood a man of Macedonia, and prayed him, saying, 'Come over into Macedonia, and help us'" (Acts 16:9). No longer would Christianity be thought of as another Asian cult. It was going to Europe, a whole different culture, a new world!

God wanted them in Macedonia all the time. But He never told them till they had proven their faith and persistence and couldn't take another step.

Keep moving—what a principle! So many people sit around waiting for that celestial crane to move them and saying, "I don't know what God wants me to do." They need to start moving so God can steer them to that area of service He has planned. Knowing God's will may mean pushing down a narrow line until you hit a dead end. At that point, God will open a door so wide, you won't be able to see around it—only through it!

What was Paul's response? It is recorded in the Book of Acts: "And after he had seen the vision, immediately we endeavored to go into Macedonia, assuredly gathering that the Lord had called us for to preach the Gospel unto them" (16:10).

Paul responded immediately and that is the only reaction when a persistent heart meets an open door.

I remember going to an amusement park

when I was a boy and paying 25¢ to get lost in a maze. It was full of mirrors, open spaces, and clear glass. The idea was to find the open spaces and make your way out of the maze. One little kid gave up and stood in one spot crying for his mother. Not I! I ran into glass and bumped into mirrors until I found the open spaces and emerged 15 minutes later.

You may bounce off a lot of closed doors, but that is God's way of forcing you into His open one. Get rolling! Be persistent.

You see, the will of God is not primarily a place. The will of God is not, first of all, for you to go there or work here. The will of God concerns you as a person. If you are the right you, you can follow your desires and you will fulfill His will.

"I beseech you therefore, brethren, by the mercies of God, that ye present your bodies a living sacrifice, holy acceptable unto God, which is your reasonable service. And be not conformed to this world, but be ye transformed by the renewing of your mind, that ye may prove what is that good and acceptable and perfect will of God" (Rom. 12:1-2).

And whatever happens in your life, along the way give thanks, for "this is the will of God in Christ Jesus concerning you" (1 Thes. 5:18). He's using it to shape you into His will.